30Days

OF

Inspiration

A PROPHETIC DEVOTIONAL

Diane Harrison

Title: Prophetic Inspirations: 30 Days of Inspiration:
A Prophetic Devotional

Copyright 2018 Diane Harrison. All rights reserved.

ISBN: 9781791504205

www.dianeharrison.ca

Contents

Acknowledgments

My thanks to Jeff and Andrea Barnhardt, for both challenging and inspiring me to write, and for their creative input.

Thank you to Jocelyn Drozda (editor), for wonderfully clarifying what I wanted to say.

Many thanks to Blaza Edwards, for always being willing to give a helping hand, and

Brian Danchuk, both friend and cover designer.

And to my family, whom I love, thank you for releasing my time so I could write.

Introduction

> *Pursue love, and desire spiritual gifts, but especially that you may prophesy ... he who prophesies speaks edification and exhortation and comfort to men.*

> 1 Corinthians 14:1, 3 (NKJV)

God's prophetic people are called to deliver His *love letters* to the world. To do so, we need to be empowered. The more *"tuned in"* we are to God, the more relevant we become to the people God wants us to influence. Engaging with a daily devotional will keep us moving forward in our prophetic gifts and alert us to the voice of the Holy Spirit as He speaks to us throughout each and every day. The Scriptures, quotes, and inspirational teachings within these pages will strengthen you in your gifting and confirm that you *are* hearing God's voice. As you interact with the daily activation responses, you will notice an increase in your awareness and sensitivity to the Holy Spirit within the thirty-day period. May you arise in strength and power to encourage and build up those in and outside the body of Christ.

Notes to Self

Hearing God's Voice

My sheep hear My voice, and I know them, and they follow me …

John 10:27 (NASB)

Developing Awareness and Sensitivity

We are created to hear God's voice. Even before becoming Christians, we have likely heard Him speak to us. We understand this to be possible because Adam could hear God speaking to him in the garden, both before and after he sinned and ate the forbidden fruit. Many times, we just don't recognize it as God, as it can be a *"still small voice."* But God is not limited; He also speaks to us through such methods as dreams, visions, Scripture, and impressions.

When we try to hear God's voice for ourselves or others, we are often unclear whether it is the voice of God or our own heart. Over time, as we become more intentional about hearing God speak to us, His voice becomes more and more distinct. For this to come to pass, we have to make ourselves available through prayer, Scripture reading, and worship—taking the time to listen to what the Lord would say to us. This helps us grow and develop in our sensitivity, and trains the ear of our heart to listen. God blesses our efforts and the Holy Spirit guides us in the development of our hearing, or *prophetic* gift. The Holy Spirit is like a cheerleader who cheers us on as we submit ourselves to growing in the Spirit. The Father loves to see us desire to learn and grow.

Activation Response

Begin with this prayer:

Father, I believe I have a deposit of the mind of Christ within me through the indwelling Holy Spirit. You have invited me to come boldly to Your throne and make my requests known to You. Lord, I am asking You to speak to me and share some of the thoughts You have toward me. I'm going to believe You and write what I hear You say to me. Let what I hear be pure and sanctified. I give You glory for what You are doing in me. I ask You now to share Your heart.

Take a minute to meditate on the Lord alone. Focus on Him. Picture Him in your mind. Know that He is thinking of you right now. He desires to share with you what He is thinking.

Begin to write. Begin to fill in whatever thoughts come to you. Do not scrutinize, just write and allow your pen to go until the words no longer come. Let your pen flow with what you hear.

Read what you have written. Ask the Lord to seal His words to you in your heart.

Day 2

An Extraordinary Life

In the last days, God says, I will pour out my Spirit on all people. Your sons and daughters will prophesy, your young men will see visions, your old men will dream dreams.

Acts 2:17 (NIV)

Developing Awareness and Sensitivity

Being hungry and desirous for the prophetic is to be commended, as we see from this Scripture. God knows that as believers we need ongoing prophetic encouragement to keep us steady and on course, moving toward the destiny He has prearranged for us.

If we can envision prophecy as *"God's love letter,"* we understand His purpose and His intense desire to communicate with us and through us. He desires to speak both individually and corporately. The prophetic person is a delivery person, bringing God's love letters to the world. What an awesome privilege!

We are to expect more prophecy in the last days, according to the prophet Joel, as quoted in Acts 2. This passage indicates there will be a dramatic increase in prophecy, dreams, and visions in the last days. We are a part of sharing God's overall plans and purposes with others. Mother Theresa sums it up so well with her famous words: *"I am a little pencil in the hands of a loving God who is sending love letters to the world."* [1]

Activation Response

Envision a bow and arrow. The arrow is a prayer of blessing designed to hit a specific target. Write out a prayer of blessing for someone you know that is on your heart and mind. Can you sense the area of a person's life for which the arrow of prayer is intended? Is it for their home, ministry, friends, workplace, or for some other area of impact? Do any pictures, Scriptures, or songs come to mind for that person? Include them in your prayer of blessing.

Share with this person all the Lord showed you, either by phone, text, email, or in person. Note their response, paying specific attention to the parts that blessed the person.

Day 3

The Purpose of Prophecy

Where there is no vision, the people perish …

Proverbs 29:18 (KJV)

Hope deferred makes the heart sick …

Proverbs 13:12a (NKJV)

Developing Awareness and Sensitivity

Prophecy is a gift from the Lord allowing us to partner with Him to strengthen, encourage, and comfort individuals or the church. As God fortifies others through prophecy, it releases His perspective of them and their lives. This helps bring the confidence they need to step into who God has called them to be, making it possible to do the things God has called them to do. Beginning to see themselves as God sees them instead of how they view themselves through the distorted lens of the world restores people's dignity and self-respect.

As you release comfort through prophetic words, hope is infused into people's lives, which gives them the fortification they need to face difficult circumstances. Prophecy can also provide insight into counseling situations, bringing people much-needed healing. As well, God's children are provided with direction and vision for their lives, with prophetic words sometimes putting them back on the right path from which they have strayed or are in danger of straying. As you consider these functions of prophecy, you will begin to understand what a high calling this is for the body of Christ!

Activation Response

Pray for one person today who you know needs comfort from the Lord, or for a person who is on your heart and mind that you feel may need comfort and encouragement.

Your faith will be built up by meditating on this Scripture:

All praise to the God and Father of our Master, Jesus the Messiah! Father of all mercy! He comes alongside us when we go through hard times, and before you know it, he brings us alongside someone else who is going through hard times so that we can be there for that person just as God was there for us. We have plenty of hard times that come from following the Messiah, but not more than the good times of his healing comfort—we get a full measure of that, too. (2 Corinthians 1:3-5 MSG)

Knowing it is God's will that you encourage others gives you confidence to step out based on this Word.

Day 4

Becoming Aware

I will lift my eyes to the mountains;
From where shall my help come?
My help comes from the LORD, who made heaven and earth.
He will not allow your foot to slip;
Behold, He who keeps Israel will neither slumber nor sleep.
The LORD is your keeper;
The LORD is your shade on your right hand.
The sun will not smite you by day,
Nor the moon by night.
The LORD will protect you from all evil;
He will keep your soul.
The LORD will guard your going out and your coming in
from this time forth and forever.

Psalm 121 (NASB)

Developing Awareness and Sensitivity

As we first tentatively venture into the realm of the prophetic, God usually focuses predominantly on one area of our gifting. As we become more proficient in hearing His voice in that manner, the Holy Spirit will increase the scope and depth of how He communicates with us. This encourages us to continually develop and keeps us dependent on the Lord—the place He want us to always be—as proclaimed in Psalm 121. As prophetic voices, we need to remain humble, refraining from the unteachable attitude of *"I have arrived,"* and know we are always growing.

Prophetic gifts can also manifest differently in certain seasons. I was introduced to prophecy through visions, then impressions. For a time, I had dreams that helped me reach out to specific people God wanted to speak to through me. No matter how God speaks to us, we can have assurance that God is interested in our spiritual and prophetic development.

9

Activation Response

Map the course of God's method of communication with you for as long as you have been aware of it. Make this a starting point and begin tracking it if this is a new experience for you.

Highlight His predominant method(s) of communication. Your chart may resemble mine. (Mine represents a 35-year time span.)

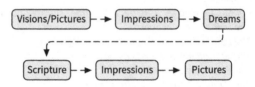

Definitions:

Dreams are moving and dynamic, occurring when we sleep. Some dreams are literal and some are symbolic, requiring an interpretation.

Pictures are static, one image, or a whole panoramic view. The picture is often a symbol to communicate a message.

Visions occur when we are awake. They can be fleeting internal pictures or pictures symbolic in nature. Open visions are like seeing something on a movie screen and are a higher level of visions.

Impressions are sometimes referred to as *"coincidences,"* but they can actually be valid prophetic impressions. Impressions are the beginning of receiving prophetic revelation. They can be of the mind, the spirit, physical, or emotional. For example, you can have an impression of pain, despair, heaviness, joy, or peace. Impressions are perceptions; sometimes we call them *"intuition."* Even though they are considered entry level revelation, they can be very significant.

Day 5

The Language of Heaven

Many, O LORD my God, are the wonders which You have done,
And Your thoughts toward us;
There is none to compare with You.
If I would declare of and speak of them,
They would be too numerous to count.

Psalm 40:5 (NASB)

Developing Awareness and Sensitivity

As we spend more and more time in the Word of God, we come to understand that learning to flow in the communication of Heaven is like studying a whole new language. It is here that we come to know the heart of God and learn how to bring Heaven to Earth. By meditating on His Word, we come to understand that God's thoughts toward every person are countless and good.

Being fluent in this language of Heaven is imperative if we are to bring His Word to others and bring hope to the nations. We need to know what God says in His Word so we can confess it and declare it, first over ourselves to strengthen our faith and embolden us to deliver the words He gives us, and then over others, to bring light into their dark world.

Activation Response

Reread Psalm 40:5 above. Ask God for one thought from His heart for you, personally.

Identify one area you are facing right now that is a challenge to you. It could be a concern such as a health challenge, anxiety over a loved one, or financial stress.

Find a Scripture that counteracts the issue you are facing. It should be a Scripture of promise and victory. Write out that Scripture and make a faith declaration over yourself.

Example: if you are experiencing fear: *"For God has not given us a spirit of fear, but of power and of love and a sound mind"* (2 Timothy 1:7). Or, try Joshua 1:9: *"Be strong and courageous. Do not be afraid, do not be discouraged, for the Lord your God will be with you wherever you go."* Is there a difference in how you feel after you use a Scripture coming in the opposite spirit of your challenge?

Day 6

Walk Up to God's Front Door

...'Thus says the LORD, the God of our father David, "I have heard your prayer, I have seen your tears; behold, I will heal you. On the third day you shall go up to the house of the LORD.

2 Kings 20:5 (NASB)

Developing Awareness and Sensitivity

Ministering effectively in the prophetic requires an anointing to prophesy. And God is the One who anoints. Thus, in order to prophesy, God and His Word must be the foundation of your life, and your relationship with Him must be intimate. To develop intimacy with the Lord requires discipline.

I had learned at the outset of my Christian walk, even before I had a prophetic ministry, that I couldn't live the life I desired without prayer and Bible reading to start my day—every day. With my strong personality, I not only had the quick Irish wit, but also the quick Irish sharp-tongue. I was afraid to leave the house without prayer and Bible reading providing a covering for me; I was unsure of how I might act or what I might say.

In reflection, recognizing this weakness in myself early on and placing my dependency on God to keep me walking straight has enabled me to lay the proper foundations in my life. Regular prayer and Bible reading are imperative to even function as a Christian. Prayer is the veritable springboard for prophecy.

13

Activation Response

God wants to communicate His thoughts to us. Listening to what He says is the basis of all prophetic expression. All believers can hear the voice of God.

As you are spending your time with Him today, listen for one thought from God's heart for one specific person. Believe God to give you a divine opportunity to share that thought with the person you have selected when the opportunity arises. If the person expresses they have received a blessing from what you shared, you can gain confidence that you are hearing from the Holy Spirit. This enables you to take the risk the next time you have a God-inspired thought for someone.

Through His Eyes

For we know in part and we prophesy in part …

1 Corinthians 13:9 (NIV)

But the one who prophesies speaks to people for their strengthening, encouraging and comfort.

1 Corinthians 14:3 (NIV)

Developing Awareness and Sensitivity

This first Scripture clearly says that when we are using the gift of prophecy, we cannot expect to be one hundred percent accurate. There is the self-part and the Holy Spirit-part to every prophecy. I believe that's why we receive the guidance of the Scripture in 1 Corinthians 14:3, revealing that the purpose of prophecy is to provide strength, comfort, and encouragement. This is actually a safety net for us to develop in prophecy and to flow in the purpose without causing confusion or harm to others. This Scripture helps us be a blessing to those we gift with prophecy, and provides us with practical advice and wisdom. It helps us develop an internal protective wisdom as well.

God challenges our motives from time to time, and as we respond appropriately with a teachable spirit, an increasingly pure flow of the prophetic is released. We want to minister in a way that is honoring to God. We want to involve our heart in the words we share with people. One of the best ways to keep our motives pure and our hearts right is to be a servant with our gift—to be other-centered, putting others ahead of ourselves.

Activation Response

Most of our activations have focused on hearing and receiving for others. Take this time for your own development. Set apart some uninterrupted time to spend with the Lord so that the fruit and gifts of the Spirit can be enriched and cultivated in His presence.

Ask God to show you things about yourself. As you practice, take note of how clearly you can hear the Lord speaking to you. Let the Holy Spirit take you to areas of greater vision for your life, which is often the desire of your heart. Also, let Him show you areas that need some love poured in—places in your heart that are dead and need life poured back into them. Meditate on seeing an image of God's true nature. Align your image with His image.

Day 8

The Functions of Prophecy

But if all prophesy, and an unbeliever or an ungifted man enters, he is convicted by all, he is called to account by all; the secrets of his heart are disclosed; and so he will fall on his face and worship God, declaring that God is certainly among you.

1 Corinthians 14:24-25 (NASB)

This command I entrust to you, Timothy, my son, in accordance with the prophecies previously made concerning you, that by them you fight the good fight…

1 Timothy 1:18 (NASB)

Praise be to the God and Father of our Lord Jesus Christ, who has blessed us in the heavenly realms with every spiritual blessing in Christ.

Ephesians 1:3 (NIV)

Developing Awareness and Sensitivity

As we further explore the functions of prophecy, we will discover that they extend beyond the body of believers, into evangelism. As the Lord reaches into hearts of those who do not know Him through prophecy, these people will come to recognize His presence and understand His love and care for them. When words that should be unknown to the speaker are released over the recipient, faith is injected into both unbelievers and believers alike, the words resonating deep within their spirits and touching their souls.

As people receive their love letters from the Lord, a spirit of thanksgiving and praise is birthed. This opens up an atmosphere ripe for the power of God to move. However, that is not the only impact; prophetic ministry provides an agenda for prayer, bringing accuracy as to where to aim its arrows. These factors make prophecy a vital part of spiritual warfare for the Lord's army.

17

As you become familiar with all the functions of prophecy, you will begin to see its value and be encouraged to pursue your gifting in this realm.

Activation Response

Try *"aiming some more arrows"* in your prayer time. See if you can sense in your heart different areas and people that need specific prayer—such as: personal growth, family, workplace, and civic and national leaders, and ministries that come to your heart and mind.

If you have a specific person to pray for, ask God for an opportunity to have a heart connection with them. See if you can target the area of concern in their heart into which you can speak. This may create an opportunity to share a dream, picture, or impression with them and a chance for you to develop your skills in listening to the still small voice of the Holy Spirit.

Day 9

The Heart of Prophecy

… *"God opposes the proud but shows favor to the humble."*

James 4:6b (NIV)

… *singing to God with gratitude in your hearts.*

Colossians 3:16b (NIV)

For the testimony of Jesus is the spirit of prophecy.

Revelation 19:10b (NKJV)

Developing Awareness and Sensitivity

"The testimony of Jesus is the spirit of prophecy;" these are the words we need to keep at the forefront of our minds as we are prophesying into people's lives. We are being asked to target specific areas of people's lives by the power of the Holy Spirit—and we need to be like Jesus as we do so. Through prophecy, healing, freedom, and deliverance can be released. Vision can be imparted. These are life-altering, life-giving opportunities.

It is through our hearts that the Holy Spirit speaks. It is an awesome honor and privilege to partner with the Holy Spirit to put a deposit of the love of Jesus into the hearts of people by delivering words, or, *love letters of prophecy*. We are being trusted with these precious hearts, and must respect the people that contain them.

This makes it essential that we practice humility daily. When we complain that life, people, and God aren't treating us right, our ability to receive His grace through humility is diminished. The result of having received undeserved grace should always be humility and gratitude, and gratitude is recognizing HE is in control.[2] We are not just growing in our gift—we are also growing in our character. Our character has to be developed to the level of our gifting for God to be able to partner with us to our fullest potential.

19

Activation Response

Talk to two people you aren't in close relationship with and purpose to get to know them. As you engage in conversation with them, ask God how He feels about them. Try to perceive the person as God does. This exercise helps to develop your ear to hear God in the middle of an everyday conversation. It also causes you to reflect on your own heart as you hear how God feels about the person. As we do this, we will find that our gift grows and our sensitivity increases.

Day 10

Growing Pains

… Walk with me and work with me—watch how I do it. Learn the unforced rhythms of grace. I won't lay anything heavy or ill-fitting on you. Keep company with me and you'll learn to live freely and lightly.

Matthew 11:28-30 (MSG)

… I dance to the tune of your revelation.

Psalm 119:70 (MSG)

Developing Awareness and Sensitivity

As we start or deepen our journey walking in prophetic ministry, patience is required, especially with ourselves. Growing is a process, and it can be an uncomfortable or even a painful one. While we are developing our ministry, God is developing our *character*. This often entails chipping away things that don't belong in our nature as we desire to emulate that of the Lord.

We need to be open to the prospect of seeking healing and growth in the areas revealed to us, including the intentional pursuit of any appropriate programs, ministries, and other available resources. As we learn to be pliable in God's hands, we can "flow to the rhythm of His grace." God needs our obedience, ensuring that He is in control—we are not to bang down doors that aren't opened for us. We need to trust God to open the right doors in *His perfect timing.* It will serve us well to remember that our gift, though public, is no more than nor less than any other gift of God. Pride is an enemy to prophetic people. Prophetic ministry *will* expose personal weakness and vulnerability. You will be refined as you face rejection and skepticism. Our humility and obedience will be tested time and again as we grow in this ministry!

21

Activation Response

Be intentional about practicing humility daily. Record the opportunities presented to you over the next week to practice humility, noting the situations and your responses. Pray for help in responding appropriately in these situations. As we do this, we will find our gift expands and our effectiveness increases.

Day 11

No Lonely Roads!

Two are better than one,
Because they have a good reward for their labor.
For if they fall, one will lift up his companion.
But woe to him who is alone when he falls,
For he has no one to help him up.

Ecclesiastes 4:9-10 (NKJV)

As iron sharpens iron,
So a man sharpens the countenance of his friend.

Proverbs 27:17 (NKJV)

Developing Awareness and Sensitivity

The road of the prophetic should *not* be a lonely one! Connecting with other prophetic people is crucial, for growth occurs as we share our common experiences and challenges, and offer encouragement and support one to another. Speaking into each other's lives, whether it be on a prophetic team or meeting together informally, affords us the necessary feedback for our development.

Maintaining unity through fellowship in the body of Christ also guards our hearts against offense and operating under a critical spirit, both of which are detrimental to the heart of prophecy. We are able to see others as Christ sees them when our hearts are overflowing with His love—not harboring past resentments and offenses.

Being active in the church, serving in whichever way the Lord has called us to do so, and displaying Christ-like behavior in our daily lives are also a part of the prophetic journey. These facets help us earn the respect and trust of those to whom we minister. Overall, we need others around us to keep our hearts right so we can effectively deliver our love letters from the Lord!

Activation Response

Do a prayerful personal inventory to determine if you have some unacknowledged or subconscious negative thoughts or feelings you are harboring. This negativity could be in reference to both people and situations, past or present. As the Lord reveals any areas of your heart, come before Him in repentance, and ask for healing. Make war on your negative thoughts. Ask the Lord if there is anyone you need to forgive, or from whom you need to ask forgiveness. Follow through on His directives, recording the outcomes.

Day 12

Speaking Intentionally

And Samuel grew, and the LORD was with him and let none of his words fall to the ground.

1 Samuel 3:19 (ESV)

Developing Awareness and Sensitivity

A recent conversation with a friend magnified the importance of the words we speak. There is weight to them; we must not underestimate the impact our words are having—both in the prophetic and in casual exchanges. Though I could not even remember what I had said to my friend a year and a half ago, all this time she had clung to the words I had shared. This spoke to me of the significance of our words, and the depth to which they can encourage others.

Through this situation, the Holy Spirit prompted me to continually be intentional about the words I used, choosing only the ones that bring life, hope, and liberty to people. We need to guard our tongues against negativity and agreeing with negativity, both in our lives and in those of others. The Lord wants us to walk in complete freedom from captivity, and deposit that same *life* into those around us.

We need to understand that our words can be veritable lifesavers to the ones the Lord brings across our path. Let us be like Samuel and grow, so that *none of our words fall to the ground.*

Activation Response

Practice being conscientious in your conversations, choosing only words that bring hope, freedom, and life to people. Make two deliberate attempts to speak encouraging words over two different people this week. Record any observations you have about these interactions.

Notes to Self

Activation Response: *What I learned*

Day 13

Love is a Command

"Let me give you a new command: Love one another. In the same way I loved you, you love one another. This is how everyone will recognize that you are my disciples—when they see the love you have for each other."

John 13:34-35 (MSG)

Developing Awareness and Sensitivity

Loving one another is not an option, but a command of Jesus. That is how the world should know we are Christians. Everything we do in our walk with the Lord must therefore be motivated by love, and function within those same borders. Ministering to others through the prophetic falls within these parameters as well. Learning to see each individual as God sees them fills us with the grace and compassion of Christ. As He is, so shall we be. As we minister through His perspective, our hearts are guarded against offense, knowing any hurtful words or actions they initiate will originate from a place of pain. We are called to carry the salve of the Lord, bringing about the healing of His people, being cautious not to cause wounding.

Practicing our gift and praying for the Lord to refine it, from the perspective of His heart, will ensure love remains at its core. If we keep our words in line with the Word of God, we will not cause confusion or offense. We want to encourage people in their faith, not play any part in them turning away from it. As Christ walked in love, so must we.

Activation Response

A word of knowledge is a specific fact about a person, place, or event that was not obtained through natural means. It could be someone's name, occupation, birthplace, birthdate, or other specific information about them. They are just facts of information. Words of knowledge show people that God knows them intimately, loves them, and cares about the details of their lives.[3] Try to recall if you have ever received a word of knowledge that fits this definition. Did you know at the time it was a word of knowledge, or did you realize it after the fact?

Ask God to give you a word of knowledge for someone and believe God for an opportunity to share it. Remember to speak with hope and grace. This can almost be like a game and you are practicing getting it right. Notice when your word is right and when it is just a guess.

Day 14

Examining Your Growth

It will come about after this
That I will pour out My Spirit on all mankind;
And your sons and daughters will prophesy,
Your old men will dream dreams,
Your young men will see visions.

Joel 2:28-29 (NASB)

Developing Awareness and Sensitivity

You will bloom and grow in your prophetic gifting! It does, however, require opportunity, awareness, and intentionality. If you find yourself battling a lack of confidence, know that you will make mistakes, and it may get messy; it is all a part of the process.

As you learn to deliver words of prophecy, are they making sense to the recipient? Don't be afraid to ask questions. Are you keeping it focused, staying within the themes that seem to be flowing at the time? Have you become more aware of what is necessary to share and what would be extraneous detail? Or are you trying to *"give them everything in one sitting,"* from words to counseling to deep intercessory prayer? Remember to give only what you have received, not expanding on it beyond what the Lord has called you to do so. (You may need to refer some people to pastoral counseling or other programs of inner healing.)

Are you keeping a positive tone, especially at the beginning and end, with any *gentle* correction sandwiched in between? Have you become adept at framing negative situations in a way that is encouraging and restorative to the recipient, rather than simply exposing their struggles?

There is a lot to consider as we develop in this gifting. It is not easy, and at times can seem overwhelming. Staying positive with faith in Jesus will keep you moving forward and keep you from getting stuck.

Activation Response

During the next opportunity you have to minister a prophetic word, be prepared to examine your session afterward, considering these growth factors. Choose one area of weakness you found and consciously try to improve upon it during a subsequent session.

Consider your non-verbal communication:

How were your mannerisms?

Is there anything you were doing that might have been interpreted as threatening or distracting? Did you remember to ask before touching or laying hands on the person?

Did you avoid any biases, including such things as race, gender, and economics?

Did you stay focused? Did you ask clarifying questions?

Did you stay within the parameters of hope, comfort, and encouragement?

Was your tone kind and restorative?

Day 15

Faith Arises

… while we look not at the things which are seen, but at the things which are not seen; for the things which are seen are temporal, but the things which are not seen are eternal.

2 Corinthians 4:18 (NASB)

Developing Awareness and Sensitivity

Evidence in Scripture of the unseen realm interacting with the natural realm is plentiful. We bear witness of angelic intervention in the accounts of Jacob's ladder (Genesis 28:12), Gideon's call to battle (Judges 6:11), and Peter's deliverance from jail (Acts 12:8). Fire falls from Heaven as Elijah calls it down in 1 Kings 18, and the hosts of Heaven are visible to the eyes of Elisha and eventually to his servant as his eyes are opened (2 Kings 6:17). Ezekiel's visions give further insight into the spiritual realm (Ezekiel 1).

The New Testament also abounds in the supernatural. Our heavenly Father approved of Jesus through an audible sound (John 12:27-30). Philip the evangelist was transported in Acts 8:39. Paul's miraculous conversion described in Acts 9 is another example, and the entire Book of Revelation is steeped in references to the unseen spiritual realm. We accept the supernatural, both as represented by the Old Testament and the New, by *faith*.

Prophecy and the ministry of the prophetic are intricately woven into and through this unseen realm. Access to it has been and will always be by *faith*. We are to use the different gifts given to us, and in the prophetic, we will prophesy in proportion to our *faith* (Romans 12:6). To develop in the prophetic requires us to grow in our faith!

As we read the Word of God and experience it becoming relevant in our daily life, our faith will increase. And as we step out in obedience and deliver the words we are called upon to give, and we witness the impact they have on the people around us, our faith will arise, taking us deeper into our relationship with Jesus and opening up the wells of the prophetic within us.

Activation Response

To grow in our faith, it is important to hide God's Word in our hearts. On separate note cards, write down a Scripture verse or two that you can memorize and meditate on for the week. Place cards where you can view them frequently: in your car, kitchen, office, and other places you will see them the most often.

Take note if the Scriptures you have been focusing on come to mind when you are giving someone a word of encouragement. To grow in prophecy, you need to grow in your Bible knowledge.

Day 16

Identity in Christ

But you are a chosen race, a royal priesthood, a holy nation, a people for God's own possession, so that you may proclaim the excellencies of Him who has called you out of darkness into His marvelous light …

1 Peter 2:9 (NASB)

For I know the plans I have for you," declares the LORD, "plans to prosper you and not to harm you, plans to give you hope and a future.

Jeremiah 29:11 (NIV)

Developing Awareness and Sensitivity

Knowing the truth of how the Lord sees you—your identity in Christ—and His vision for your life are essential if you are to accurately represent His perception of others through you. The deeper we understand who we are and the Lord's thoughts about us, the better we can portray His love and vision for others.

His thoughts toward you are good. You are chosen. You have received good gifts from the Lord. In Christ, you are righteous and holy—a masterpiece. His intentions toward you are good. His plans and purposes for you are good. Condemning thoughts and beliefs about yourself are not from God; they are arrows of the enemy. Know who you are and whose you are. Know His blood covers all, and speak out the truth over your life.

"The two most important days in your life are the day you were born and the day you found out why."

—Mark Twain

Activation Response

Reflect on how you speak about yourself. Record your thoughts.

Speak out loud that you are prophetically gifted. Receive this truth.

Name two more giftings that God has given you. Thank Him for those giftings.

Write out a prophetic blessing and make that a declaration over your life. Repeat it out loud—often.

Focus on aspects of the Spirit and rejoice in the gifts that are given to you.

Day 17

Spiritual Discernment

But a natural man does not accept the things of the Spirit of God, for they are foolishness to him; and he cannot understand them, because they are spiritually appraised.

1 Corinthians 2:14 (NASB)

Developing Awareness and Sensitivity

Discernment: God-inspired identification of an unseen spiritual reality. We receive it by hearing from God. All discernment is based on perceiving from God the variables of good versus evil in any given area of life. All of Heaven can be discerned as well as the things of this Earth.[4]

The *gift of discerning of spirits* is a supernatural ability which operates to give *spiritual discernment* (sharp perceptions and understandings of what is transpiring in the spiritual realm). This enables us to make sound biblical judgments and decisions. This gift gives spiritual discernment in four areas:

a) the work of the Holy Spirit in such areas as prophecy, visions, dreams, signs, wonders, and bringing people to salvation (Acts 2:14-21)

b) the work of the demonic, affording us power in such things as recognizing and casting out demonic spirits (Acts 16:16-18, Luke 13:11-13)

c) the work of the human spirit, leading us to know the inner workings of man's heart (Acts 8:18-23)

d) the work of angelic beings, allowing us to have visions and interact with angelic beings (Acts 10:1-6).

As we learn to walk deeper in the ministry of the prophetic, an increase in discernment of spirits is crucial. We need to scrutinize

35

and ask questions, searching out biblical truth. Discernment needs to be tested, just as with other spiritual gifts.

Activation Response

Ask the Lord to bring to mind a recent situation in which you exercised spiritual discernment. (If nothing comes to mind, watch for the next situation that arises and apply the following tests. Continue using these tests as you progress in your walk and in your discernment.)

Apply each of these five tests of spiritual discernment to your situation.

a) Does your discernment agree with Scripture?

b) What is the ongoing fruit of your discernment?

c) Are you relying upon the inner anointing of the Spirit to lead you into truth? Check that your discernment isn't being hindered through such things as wrong doctrine or other biased influences.

d) Is the peace of Christ ruling in your heart in what you are discerning?

e) Is your discernment consistent with the heart, nature, and character of God?

Day 18

Upgrade Your Spiritual Life

But what happens when we live God's way? He brings gifts into our lives, much the same way that fruit appears in an orchard—things like affection for others, exuberance about life, serenity. We develop a willingness to stick with things, a sense of compassion in the heart, and a conviction that a basic holiness permeates things and people. We find ourselves involved in loyal commitments, not needing to force our way in life …

Gal 5:22-23 (MSG)

Developing Awareness and Sensitivity

This Scripture is describing the fruit that begins to appear in our lives as we become intentional God-seekers. When we go on a quest to build our spiritual lives, or *muscles*, we should begin to see noticeable changes such as:

1. A new heightened awareness of the spiritual dimension.

2. We pray differently. Instead of begging God for things, we begin to act more like a son or daughter.

3. We have more passion and vision, not just for our own life but for others as well.

4. We are able to take more risks.

5. We become more excited about God's divine plans and the divine appointments with people He brings across our path.

6. We are *"more available"* to God.

7. We have a new peace and contentment. We understand that life circumstances are exactly designed for us to grow and reap the benefits.

Activation Response

Take this week to process today's Scripture. Ask the Holy Spirit to teach you as you read, reread, pray, sit still, listen, and think. Write down your thoughts. In your journal, record the truths God is teaching you. Write a letter with promises and upgrades in the Lord you want to claim.

Day 19

Through the Looking Glass

So we're not giving up. How could we! Even though on the outside it often looks like things are falling apart on us, on the inside, where God is making new life, not a day goes by without his unfolding grace. These hard times are small potatoes compared to the coming good times, the lavish celebration prepared for us. There's far more here than meets the eye. The things we see now are here today, gone tomorrow. But the things we can't see now will last forever.

2 Corinthians 4:16-18 (MSG)

Developing Awareness and Sensitivity

We are a spirit that lives in a fallen human body in the natural realm. However, through the redemption of Christ, we have been given the choice to live in the spiritual realm. Like Jesus, we can operate from one while living in the other. Our focus will determine out of which realm we ultimately live. The Bible tells us we are to live by faith not by sight (2 Corinthians 5:7), which indicates the spiritual realm. But faith is not blind. Faith sees—extraordinarily clearly—like peering through a looking glass. Which world do you live from? The natural, in the state of fallen man? Or the spiritual, as redeemed man?

Heaven is right here, and as a child of God we can reach into Heaven anytime, like drinking water from a well, and draw upon all the things to which He has given us access: things like gifts of the Spirit and fruits of the Spirit (love and patience!) Most of all, we can procure a higher perspective—that of the Spirit. It is available to us. This aspect is crucial, as most of our success in life depends on how we think: *"For as he thinks in his heart, so is he ..."* (Proverbs 23:7a NKJV). Though there are many times we cannot directly change our circumstances, we can change our perspective. (These thoughts are credited to Tim Harrison's *Hunger House* class.)

Activation Response

So where are most of your thoughts directed? Are you consumed with *natural earth,* or *spiritual Heaven?* Do you desire to live from a spiritual realm? Pray and ask the Holy Spirit to teach you how to live in the spiritual realm.

Meditate on Colossians 3:2: *"Set your minds on things above, not on earthly things"* (NIV), and

Romans 12:2b, *"...be transformed by the renewing of your mind ..."* (NASB).

Write out some promises that come to mind as you declare these Scriptures over your life.

Day 20

Growing Through Feedback

Pursue love, and desire spiritual gifts, but especially that you may prophesy.

1 Corinthians 14:1 (NKJV)

Developing Awareness and Sensitivity

As a prophetic person, the best way I know how to grow in the gift is through *feedback*. This is why it is important to have or form a group where you can *"practice prophecy."* Growth doesn't happen through theory, but through practice. Of course, prophetic guidelines and etiquette are important to learn so your gift flourishes in the right setting, but if you never actually practice, you don't grow.

When you take the risk to share a word, the positive response of the person or group are good indicators of your accuracy, and it confirms you are *"hearing"* the voice of the Holy Spirit. This confirmation received builds confidence and a desire to prophesy more, and ultimately causes growth in your gifting. Feedback through confirmation, especially of accuracy, never gets old and always increases boldness. At the same time, we can't place all our confidence in feedback; we may not always have the opportunity to receive it. As you mature in prophetic gifting, you gain trust that the Holy Spirit is speaking and working through you.

Activation Response

Choose a person in your vicinity and ask God to speak to you about them.

Write down any information you feel you are receiving from the Holy Spirit. Take a risk and share the information. Ask them if anything you shared was accurate. Notice if your feelings of confidence are heightened by this feedback.

Notes to Self

Activation Response: *What I learned*

Day 21

Google God

Where there is no vision, the people perish …

Proverbs 29:18 (KJV)

Blessed are those whose strength is in you, whose hearts are set on pilgrimage. As they pass through the valley of Baka, they make it a place of springs; the autumn rains also cover it with pools. They go from strength to strength, till each appears before God in Zion.

Psalm 84:5-7 (NIV)

Developing Awareness and Sensitivity

Many people believe prophecy will help them find the will of God for their lives. In their minds, if they could just *"get a word,"* a tough decision would become much easier. *Should I take this job? Marry this person? Go on that mission trip?* In fact, prophecy is very much linked to discovering God's will for your life, but the way it operates is quite different than many imagine.

When God speaks destiny into your life through a prophetic word, it typically starts a journey that can be long, distressing, and usually leads to significant change in your life. You have to approach destiny like a pilgrimage in which you cannot see the end of the path you are to walk. There will be many twists and turns along the way, perhaps even some setbacks, but you'll arrive if you persevere—keeping your eyes on Jesus, the author and perfector of our faith (Hebrews 12:2 NASB).

There are certainly times that God will speak prophetically into the details of daily life, but most often God speaks to the big picture— your destiny. Once a person understands their destiny, which I would define as *"God's vision and purpose for their life,"* it becomes much easier to make the day to day decisions.

Activation Response

As you become more aware of God speaking to you, write down each time you hear His voice during the day or night. Remember, God wants to communicate with us, and it's not just when we have our prayer or devotion time set aside. The Holy Spirit wants to be our companion and is with us all throughout the day and night.

Determine if you can see some of the *"puzzle pieces"* of your life begin to fit together as God leads you on your journey. Use these revelations to help you persevere when the road you are walking becomes difficult.

Day 22

Sharpening Your Sensitivity

Now Samuel did not yet know the LORD, nor had the word of the LORD yet been revealed to him. So the LORD called Samuel again for the third time. And he arose and went to Eli and said, "Here I am, for you called me." Then Eli discerned that the LORD was calling the boy. And Eli said to Samuel, "Go lie down, and it shall be if He calls you, that you shall say, 'Speak, LORD, for Your servant is listening.' " So Samuel went and lay down in his place. Then the LORD came and stood and called as at other times, "Samuel! Samuel!" And Samuel said, "Speak, for Your servant is listening."

1 Samuel 3:7-10 (NASB)

Developing Awareness and Sensitivity

Many times, we are unaware of the voice of God as He vies for our attention over the din of our daily lives. Unfamiliarity with His ways of communicating increases our chance of missing His call. We therefore need to continually sharpen our sensitivity to the ways God speaks in communicating prophetic revelation.

Deeper prophetic insight develops through intentional, directed practice in increasing sensitivity. As we spend time with the Lord and are conscious of taking the time to listen, really listen, we not only foster the intimacy of our relationship, but also our awareness and sensitivity to His voice in our daily lives.

Activation Response

Begin in prayer, asking the Lord what He would say. Use the checklist below to perform a check on any insights you believe are coming from the Holy Spirit. Record any sensations, impressions, visions, etc., regardless of how gently or softly it comes to you. If you are struggling to hear clearly, return to an attitude of rest before the Lord. Continue to periodically complete the inventory as you feel your repertoire expanding.

1. Impressions:
   a) Thoughts
   b) Sensations
   c) Emotional feelings

2. Spiritual Senses:
   a) Seeing
   b) Hearing
   c) Touching or Feeling

3. The Voice of the Lord:
   a) Still small voice
   b) internal audible voice (your conscience)

4. Visions or pictures:

Day 23

Claim Your Upgrades

'And it shall be in the last days,' God says, 'that I will pour forth of My spirit on all mankind; and your sons and your daughters shall prophesy, and your young men shall see visions, and your old men shall dream dreams; even on my bondslaves, both men and women, I will in those days pour forth of My spirit And they shall prophesy.

Act 2:17-18 (NASB)

Developing Awareness and Sensitivity

These are days when God is raising up a new level of prophets and those with prophetic gifting. We can expect to see people with an increased interest and desire to prophesy, and that children will enter into prophetic gifting. There is a new flavor of prophets who, like Shadrach, Meshach, and Abednego have been called to purity, holiness, and anointing from their youth. God wants them to be fearless and walk naturally on a spiritual plane of living supernaturally. God's desire is for the prophetic to infiltrate and influence all levels of our culture and society.

In the meantime, He is calling mothers and fathers to take their place in mentoring and developing prophetic people. Prophetic people are to be credible and a stabilizing force in our communities. Being pillars for a lost world goes hand in hand with a greater thrust into the harvest.

Activation Response

God often speaks to believers through dreams. Search the Scriptures to find an example of a dream that is:

1. literal (Matthew 1:20)

2. symbolic (Genesis 28:12)

3. angelic/God (Matthew 2:13, Luke 1:11, 19, 26)

Can you identify a time where you have had one of these types of dreams?

What did you learn? Was the Lord leading you to take action?

What was the result?

Day 24

Delight is a Practice

… But I delight in Your law.

Psalm 119:70b (NASB)

Delight yourself in the LORD;
And He will give you the desires of your heart.

Psalm 37:4 (NASB)

Developing Awareness and Sensitivity

Much is written and discussed about the *joy* of the Lord, but the concept of *delighting in Him,* a deeper aspect of this area, is not as prevalent. Our delight in the Lord should be like that of a parent or grandparent at the birth of a child. This delight stems from the very essence of *who* they are—who God has made them to be—not by what they have done or have given us. The flood of pure joy washing over one's heart because of the existence of this child is to be the same delight we are to have in God, who is awesome in His grace and majesty.

The converse is also true—the Lord takes this same delight in us as His children, and we are to receive it. We are intensely aware of our faults and failures, yet the Lord looks upon us with pure delight, as He sees us through the blood of Jesus. Or, as Jonathon Hessler expresses it, *"Jesus sees us through the holes in His hands."* Zephaniah 3:17 also reveals the heart of God toward us: He rejoices over us with singing.

As we practice delight, He will give us the desires of our heart and lead us to walk in the giftings and callings He has put within us, even taking us to other people groups throughout the earth. As we fulfill the purposes for which He has created us, walking in our true identity, it is then that the deep wells of joy are released. As these wells of joy are accessed, we can be the vessel God uses to teach others to do the same.

Activation Response

Meditate on today's Scripture. Record the nature and some of the aspects of God in which you take delight. Allow the Holy Spirit to help you savor this delight in the Lord. Ask for help to accept the Lord's delight over you. Ask Him specifically how He sees you. Write several adjectives that express how God sees you. (For example: loving, careful, teachable, hungry for His presence, committed, etc.) Use God's lens to describe His delight over you.

Day 25

Sharpen Your Perceptions

Let two or three prophets speak [as inspired by the Holy Spirit], while the rest pay attention and weigh carefully what is said.

1 Corinthians 14:29 (AMP)

Be devoted to one another in brotherly love; give preference to one another in honor; not lagging behind in diligence, fervent in spirit, serving the Lord; rejoicing in hope, persevering in tribulation, devoted to prayer, contributing to the needs of the saints, practicing hospitality.

Romans 12:10-13 (NASB)

Developing Awareness and Sensitivity

Sometimes prophecy isn't received, not because it's scary or spooky, but because people haven't witnessed the use of respectful manners in its delivery. Personal words should be shared in private settings, rather than in front of a crowd or group. Respectful tones and an appropriate volume should be used in the delivery of a prophecy.

An alternative to delivering a word orally could be to write it out for the person in a card of encouragement. Your tone should still be one of blessing—that's the Lord's heart toward them: *"The spirit of Jesus is the spirit of prophecy,"* and it's His heart that we should be communicating. We want to use words and terminology that are redemptive. God wants to draw us toward Himself. It's the love of God that draws us to repentance (Romans 2:4). We want to prophesy hope, even in difficult areas, and speak to people about a path to freedom. God always desires restoration, offering a path to a more intimate relationship with Him.

Activation Response

As we live with a human soul, sometimes we struggle to keep our heart and tone redemptive. I have found a practice which has become a discipline to keep my thinking positive and moving forward. I listen to messages, podcasts, and YouTube videos of speakers from all over the world who are known for their positivity and are known visionaries.

Choose a person or people you know to deliver positive and encouraging messages (e.g. Steven Furtick, Bill Johnson, Joyce Meyers, Graham Cooke, Kris Vallotton). Purpose to listen to them for one week, one message per day. Do you notice your thoughts and attitude becoming more consistently positive? Does your own spirit feel uplifted?

Day 26

Going the Distance

So I sent messengers to them, saying, "I am doing a great work and I cannot come down. Why should the work stop while I leave it and come down to you?" They sent messages to me four times in this manner, and I answered them in the same way.

Nehemiah 6:3-4 (NASB)

Developing Awareness and Sensitivity

Every day we are faced with opportunities that have the potential to distract us from the Lord's calling on our lives. These distractions shift and change as we progress through different stages of life. From financial pressure to the weariness of parenting young children, to marital problems, feeling a lack of support for your ministry or giftings, feeling invisible, facing identity crises, wading through life's many disappointments, maneuvering through the heartache of wayward children, and suffering grief and loss are but a few of the myriad of issues we contend with at any given time.

Adding to these negative distractions are all the *good opportunities* and obligations in which we feel pressured to partake. Job or career opportunities are often a priority. Added to these are the relational, vacation, entertainment, and even religious distractors that can be factored in. Our buckets are more than overflowing. Eventually, we need to come to realize that we have to say *no* to good things, so we aren't distracted from the *best* things—the things that connect us to our vision and the calling of God. We must not allow these *good opportunities* to detract from God's ultimate direction and plan for our lives.

Our families and marriages are undeniably a part of God's calling, and must be given a place among our top priorities, along with our ministries. Events, organizations, and excess hobbies and recreation are not obligations and may need to be released at times. You will have to actively fight for and guard your mandates from God. As you attempt to squeeze just one more activity into an already overtaxed schedule, just whisper *"I am doing a great work and I cannot come down."*

Activation Response

Examine Jeremiah 29:11-14a (NIV).

"For I know the plans I have for you," declares the LORD, "plans to prosper you and not to harm you, plans to give you hope and a future. Then you will call on me and come and pray to me, and I will listen to you. You will seek me and find me when you seek me with all your heart. I will be found by you, declares the LORD …"

See yourself as God sees you, elevated to His strength and power. Call on Him; seek Him. Listen to what He says about you and His plans for you. Don't feel you have to rush—this is practicing knowing the Presence of the Lord.

Write out key words, phrases, and ideas from the Scripture. Write out your personal thoughts about each and apply them to your own life. Do you need to reorganize your priorities in any areas to follow more closely the plans of God? Have you been tempted by distractions? Are there any *good* things you need to forfeit so you are able to pursue the *great* things?

Day 27

Examining Your Fruit

You will know them by their fruits. Do men gather grapes from thorn bushes or figs from thistles? Even so, every good tree bears good fruit, but a bad tree bears bad fruit.

Matthew 7:16-17 (NKJV)

And though I have the gift of prophecy, and understand all mysteries and all knowledge, and though I have all faith, so that I could remove mountains, but have not love, I am nothing.

1 Corinthians 13:2 (NKJV)

" … so that you may live a life worthy of the Lord and please him in every way: bearing fruit in every good work, growing in the knowledge of God, being strengthened with all power according to his glorious might so that you may have great endurance and patience …

Colossians 1:10-11 (NIV)

Developing Awareness and Sensitivity

It cannot be restated too often: prophetic people must display true prophetic character—an example to the ones to whom we minister. We need to check our hearts … often. What is your motivation? *Love* must be the continual motivation, not a need to be noticed. If the latter motivation creeps in, it is time for a heart check, and the removal of any arrows the enemy has successfully lodged underneath your armor.

False motivation can corrupt your fruit. We need to constantly ask ourselves, *"What are the fruits of my ministry? Unity, harmony, peace, or division, strife, and discord?"* A spirit of independence can lead us to believe we know it all—a dangerous place for a prophet! No one person receives the full picture. We each have a piece of the puzzle; a piece of the bigger picture: *"We know in part and we prophesy in part"* (1 Corinthians 13:9 ESV).

Walking in the steps of a prophetic gifting requires us to be held in a position of accountability, within a group of like-minded people, and under authority of leadership. A healthy relationship with other members of the body of Christ will reflect our relationship with Christ, and ensure others we can be trusted with the delicate parts of their heart as we minister prophetically to them.

Activation Response

By reflecting on your experiences, you will initiate healthy growth. One area to self-evaluate is how well you are fitting into the team of prophetic people around you.

Are you proving yourself a team-player, staying within any guidelines laid out?

Do you tend to monopolize, or should you speak out a little more?

Are you showing yourself trustworthy to your church leadership?

Are you coming under the authority of your leaders?

Day 28

Flavor of Gifting

And He gave some as apostles, and some as prophets, and some as evangelists, and some as pastors and teachers, for the equipping of the saints for the work of service, to the building up of the body of Christ, until we all attain to the unity of the faith, and of the knowledge of the Son of God, to a mature man, to the measure of the stature which belongs to the fullness of Christ.

Ephesians 4:11-13 (NASB)

Developing Awareness and Sensitivity

No two prophetic people function exactly alike. Each has a unique *flavor* in his or her gifting. Some people have an intercessory flavor, which leads to prophetic prayer. Others are evangelistic. Still others are more predictive in their approach. Some flow better in personal prophecy over an individual, while others feel led to deliver God's messages to groups of people.

The prophetic gift is the same for each person; it just manifests in different ways. We thus want to celebrate our uniqueness of gifting rather than trying to conform to another person's style. Paul emphasized this in 1 Corinthians 12:4, when the Corinthians thought they were praying to many different gods: *"There are diversities of gifts, but the same Spirit"* (NKJV). He desired to have them understand there was only one God and one Holy Spirit, just functioning differently in each person.

We are given more of God's grace to flow in the area He has designed for us. Since grace has different flavors, we therefore have different flavors of gifting. There is an Apostolic grace, a Pastoral grace, grace for Teachers and Evangelists, and a Prophetic grace. We exercise our gifts according to the level of our grace; thus, you will have the most grace to function in your personal gifting style.

Activation Response

Take a few moments to ponder in which area you feel the most connected or the stirring to connect. Can you identify what your flavor of gifting is? Are you more drawn toward prayer, outreach, teaching, personal or group prophecy?

For confirmation, approach a few friends who can help by sharing with you their observations and impressions of your gifting. Many times, our giftings are more easily identified by others than by ourselves.

Day 29

Act on What You Hear

Every desirable and beneficial gift comes out of heaven. The gifts are rivers of light cascading down from the Father of Light.

James 1:17 (MSG)

… Lead with your ears, follow up with your tongue, and let anger straggle along in the rear.

James 1:19 (MSG)

In simple humility, let our gardener, God, landscape you with the Word, making a salvation-garden of your life. Don't fool yourself into thinking that you are a listener when you are anything but, letting the Word go in one ear and out the other. Act on what you hear!

James 1:21-23 (MSG)

Developing Awareness and Sensitivity

Learning to prophesy is dependent on training our spiritual ear to listen. These passages challenge us to learn to grow in listening to the Holy Spirit. In the book of Revelation, chapter 2, there is an appeal to each of the churches to *"Listen to the wind words of the Spirit."* This provides a strong analogy: the Holy Spirit is like a wind, that if we perk up our ears, we can hear what the wind (Holy Spirit) is saying. If we don't pay attention, it blows right past us: *"in one ear and out the other."*

The second challenge in the passages from James is to *"act on what you hear,"* and this requires *faith*—both to have confidence that your hearing is accurate, and to act on what you hear. Do you have the faith to call a friend you have been thinking about? Or the faith to write a note of encouragement to someone? Do you have enough faith to pursue God in your daily life? There is a wonderful story

59

about Samuel, where he learns to discern the voice of God speaking to him. He too, had to learn to hear the voice of the Father. Read 1 Samuel 3:1-10.

"… we must never forget that the highest appreciation is not to utter words, but to live by them."

—John F. Kennedy

Activation Response

Ask God to speak to you specifically about a friend or family member. Begin to write down what you hear. Record every thought that comes to you. Do not overthink or analyze what you have written, just write until thoughts no longer come to mind. Let your pen be your voice. If there is a pause, ask the Lord if He has anything else He wants to say to you about that person.

Now you can bless the person by sharing what the Lord told you:

Share your word with the person by phone, if possible, so you can request feedback. Ask them if your word was helpful and encouraging.

(Did what you shared make sense and did it speak to them in a specific area?)

Day 30

Developing a Lifestyle of Risk

God doesn't want us to be shy with His gifts, but bold and loving and sensible.

2 Tim 1:7 (MSG)

Developing Awareness and Sensitivity

When you recognize you have a prophetic gift, you quickly become aware of the constant challenge to take risks. The Holy Spirit nudges us to do things outside of our comfort zones through such methods as words, visions, dreams, and impressions. We begin to test whether or not we have heard correctly as we execute His direction through these promptings. Our confidence and excitement grow when positive feedback is received, helping prepare us for the next opportunity.

Before the step of obedience is taken, you may feel like you are on the top of a cliff, deciding whether or not to jump. Abandoning your thoughts of, *This is ridiculous. I'm making this up, you jump*—(or get gently *pushed off!*)

Risk can become almost a daily prompt from the Holy Spirit. We can decide to battle against these nudges, or we can decide to take the risk and grow. As we step out in this arena, the challenges expand, but so does our confidence in our ability to hear. Before long, we are living a LIFESTYLE of risk and we have entered into a training contract with the Holy Spirit. On our part, the contract requires being willing to become a fool for Jesus, surrendering to the knowledge that the Holy Spirit's ways are best, and dying to self. On the other side of the contract, we gain by deepening our trust that the Lord will care for us if we keep our hearts humble before Him. We also welcome a life of blessing as we flourish in our gift and in the fruitfulness of a life given away.

Activation Response

Identify your fears of *"taking risks"* through prophecy. If there is a lack of freedom when you think about yourself, ask the Holy Spirit to reveal the lie that is binding you. Review what God believes about you.

Identify times where you have taken risks and received blessings. Record your observations. Analyze what you have learned about taking risks.

A Final Word

I pray that through this devotional, you have become more sensitive to hearing God's voice and have grown in your prophetic gifting. As you faced each daily response, I pray it stretched and challenged you, allowing you to hear the heart of the Lord for yourself and for others more effectively. Continue to apply what you have learned as you go forth on your journey, sharing God's love for His people wherever He leads you to go.

I pray you have been able to step out in your faith, take risks, and venture deep into the Lord, examining the motives of your heart and responding as He shaped and molded you, and continues to do so. And I pray that now, at the end of the thirty days, you will see the evidence of fruitfulness in your life, and that this fruitfulness will continue to increase. Be blessed, and may the Lord meet you in your desire to grow!

In my visions now before me,
Anoint my eyes with salve to see.
Then I will know You and Your ways,
I will see You face to face.
The darkness flees in Your presence,
Your light is sown with Heaven's scent.
It's You revealing mysteries
And I shall know Your majesty.

—Linda Wilson

Endnotes

1. Mother Theresa. "Inspirational Quotes." Goodreads. *https://goodreads.com* (accessed November 11, 2018).

2. Dye, Michael. *The Church: Helping or Hurting.* Rose Island Bookworks, 2014, p. 215.

3. Thompson, Steve. You May All Prophesy Study Guide. Fortmills: Morningstar Publications, 2008.

4. Bolz, Shawn. God Secrets Workbook. Studio City: ICreate Productions, 2017, p.125

5. Cooke, Graham. *The Newness Advantage.* Vancouver: Brilliant Book House, 2017

6. Harrison, Diane. Prophetic Team Workbook, Instructor Guide. Amazon, 2018

7. Poem by Linda Wilson (slwilson@sasktel.net)

About the Author

Diane Harrison has a ministry of teaching and equipping prophetic people and prophetic teams. She minsters in local churches in Canada, USA, and other countries, sharing a model she has developed for prophetic teams. Currently she coordinates prophetic teams at Harvest City Church and works with churches within the Lifelinks organization. Her desire is to see people equipped and flowing in their gifting and destiny. You can find her book *The Power of Prophetic Teams* and the accompanying workbook *Power of Prophetic Teams* on Amazon. You can also contact her at www.dianeharrison.ca

Notes to Self

Activation Response: *What I learned*